We then embarked on field work to study the rock strata of Doncaster. We took hand lenses and studied the lithology of the rocks at Barnburgh Cliff, Cedar Road in Balby and Warmsworth Park. Looking at local rock formations meant we could gain a much more secure understanding on the strata of Doncaster. We studied in detail how you could see signs of biological weathering (caused by plants or animals) and mechanical weathering (caused by frozen water).

We then did a historical enquiry, studying Doncaster's mining past and looking in detail at Harworth mine on the Nottinghamshire border. Focusing on the Harworth case study gave us an insight into a successful mine in Doncaster. We discovered some of the more interesting aspects of Harworth's story, such as the initial investment from Germany to sink the pits and the tensions that followed during the outbreak of the First World War. We were also surprised to learn how an entire community sprang up from the sinking of Harworth; Bircotes village having been built specifically to house workers from the pit. We also saw, for the first time, how the closure of a mine affected the local community.

In Maths, we looked at the perimeter and area of the site at Harworth to understand the sheer scale of the colliery, and how it must have dominated the landscape at that time.

Throughout the learning expedition we studied 'Kit's Wilderness' by David Almond. This text is about a small mining community in the fictional town of Stoneygate in Northumberland. The main characters are a group of children, whose ancestors worked down the pit for generations and how they begin to see the ghosts of long-gone boys from pit disasters. This book taught us more about how pit closures changed the communities and how for some pit villagers, coal was all they had or knew. In the story Kit's Grandfather was a miner, and he told Kit numerous stories from his time as a collier. This is similar to the responsibility we now feel for keeping Doncaster's mining heritage alive because unless these stories are told and retold, they could be lost forever.

FOREWORD

In producing this book, we have interviewed numerous experts from former mining communities in Doncaster including ex-miners, a 'strike baby' and women who were pivotal in the efforts during the strike as members of 'Women against pit closures'. This taught us about the life of our mining communities first hand and provided us with stories that enriched our understanding, ultimately helping us to answer our guiding question.

We discovered that although many would say that the British people owe the miners a great amount, there are those who would disagree; for instance, the Government at the time of the 1984 strike. This is despite the fact that mining gave Britain a lot during the wars, and the Bevin Boys prevented inevitable disaster for our country. The strikes and blackouts that followed the 1970s undoubtedly contributed to the view in Margaret Thatcher's government, that the pit workers were expendable and that it was in Britain's interest to close the collieries. We found that many people would say that although the strikes and blackouts caused great disruption, the miners were fighting for their rights and what they believed in; something that not all communities can say that they have done.

Each one of us has contributed to this book: with our understanding of the geology of Doncaster and why the mines came to be here; with the industrial and social histories that we have discovered; with the artwork that we have been inspired to create and with the stories that have compelled us to share and pass on, so that they might live on forever.

Year 7 Students

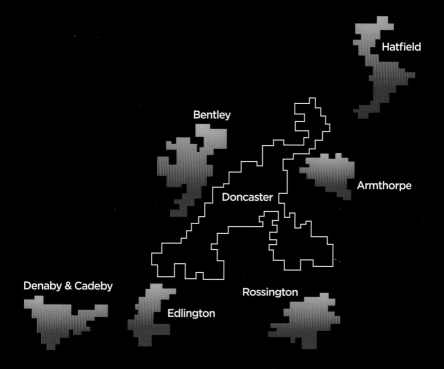

Hatfield

Bentley

Doncaster

Armthorpe

Denaby & Cadeby

Rossington

Edlington

DONCASTER
THE GEOLOGY

Doncaster's Strata

There are three main strata found near the surface in and around Doncaster. The first stratum, found in the far east of the borough, is the Coal Measures. This means that Doncaster is located in what was the South Yorkshire coalfield. The second stratum is the Magnesium Limestone which is found in the west of Doncaster. The sediment from dead sea creatures left behind this unique stratum of dolomitic (calcium magnesium carbonate) limestone, which is all that remains of the ancient Zechstein Sea. Finally, in the east there is red sandstone.

The Coal Measures

The oldest rocks in and around Doncaster are the Coal Measures. In 1914 in Barnburgh a borehole was drilled down to 720m though the Coal Measures. As well as coal, this borehole found sandstone, siltstone, mudstones and ironstone.

These rocks were laid down 310 million years ago when the area was a swamp. The seams of coal formed when plants in the swamp died and then as the organic material decayed it became a soil called peat. This was later compacted and cemented by layers of new sediment above. Over millions of years as the soil was buried, the resulting heat and the pressure caused chemicals such as nitrogen and hydrogen to be removed from the peat, leaving behind the carbon which forms the coal.

The stratum contains many seams of coal in layers between sandstone, siltstone and mudstones. In the late Carboniferous period the sea level changed frequently. As the sea level changed it deposited sediments such as sand and silt which became different rock formations in the Coal Measures. For example, the shale was formed from deep water depositing silt and clay. The sandstone was formed from river deltas depositing sand. Finally, the coal represents the forest and swamps.

Magnesium Limestone

Magnesium limestone is found in the west of Doncaster. The magnesium limestone was formed during the Permian Period which was 251 to 271 million years ago. During this time what is now Doncaster was below a shallow tropical sea as Britain was nearer to the equator at that time.
Calcium carbonate from the shells of dead sea creatures formed a lime-rich mud. Over millions of years this sediment was lithified to create the limestone.

Red Sandstone

The red sandstone in Doncaster is part of the Sherwood Sandstone Group and is the youngest stratum in Doncaster. These rocks come from the Triassic Period around 200-250 million years ago. What is now the red sandstone was found in a desert with braided rivers running through it. The red sandstone and bands of marl are formed from grains of sand and clay.

To form the red sandstone, the river had to be flowing fast to carry and then deposit the sand. However, when the water was flowing more slowly, such as during overbank floods or during the formation of lakes, it would have deposited the clay to form the bands of red marl. This stratum is also a very important aquifer, from which we get much of our drinking water. It is the second biggest aquifer in the UK after chalk. The porosity of this stratum led to lots of problems with water in many of the mines around Doncaster.

Written by Tyler, Leighton, Bradley, Sophie, Tiggy, Josh, Logan, Tuscany, Harley and Rhys

Mining in Doncaster

In Doncaster, the rock strata dip to the east. This is because of movement in the tectonic plates. Millions of years ago they pushed up what are now the Pennines. This means that mines in the east of Doncaster have deeper shafts because they had to go though more materials to get down to the coal seams.

The Barnsley Seam was the richest of the seams. It was the thickest and had the best quality coal. So every mine in Doncaster was sunk to this seam and did not tend to work any seams below as it was very expensive to drill further down. Roadways were then drilled from the pit bottoms, following the seam.

These roadways were sometimes miles long. There were some problems with faults in Doncaster. For example, in Edlington, the mine was deeper than might have been expected. This is because the mine lay between the North and South Don faults. A fault is when the rock breaks and the two sections either side move in relation to each other. Before the rocks dipped to the east, tectonic movements caused a huge slab of rock where Edlington is now, to move down. In some mines, the seam would disappear as the roadways had hit a fault. In addition, some mines such as Edlington also had lots of problems with methane gas, which had to be pumped out. At Edlington, so much gas was pumped out that they were able to sell the gas to increase their profits.

Mining in Doncaster reached its peak in the middle of the 20th century, with most mines closed by the end of the century. For example in 1927 at Rossington Main there were 2000 men underground and 500 men on the surface. By 2006, following problems with faulting in the area being worked, the pit had closed.

The last active pit in Doncaster was Hatfield Main which finally closed in 2015. The two headgears and some of the surface buildings are still standing and are the last reminder of a different world that must not be forgotten.

MARKHAM MAIN
HISTORY

Armthorpe is situated in the north east of Doncaster. The Armthorpe settlement was first recorded in 1086 after the Viking invasion and was known as Ernulfestorp. Armthorpe was recorded in the Domesday Book as being the property of the monks of Roche Abbey near Maltby, who had a grange there.

Before the sinking of the pits Armthorpe was originally farmland, woodlands and orchards. In June 1913 Earl Fitzwilliam leased the minerals under his Armthorpe Estate to Sir Arthur Markham. The first shaft was sunk on 6th May 1916 and was 865 metres deep, both the shafts were 5.2 metres in diameter.

On the 24th of August 1916, mining stopped due to the First World War. Sinking was briefly resumed in 1919, but was suspended until 21st May 1922. Both shafts reached the Barnsley seam, at a depth of 668.5 metres and the first lot of coal was recovered in May 1924.

In World War Two, the Germans tried to bomb Markham Main Colliery, but failed. After the plane crash landed, the gunner ran down Paxton Crescent and shot at the doors.

For many years Markham Main was used as a place to train new miners, as it had a training tunnel.

In 1934, the first conveyor was introduced on a longwall advancing face. Previous to this, the coal was worked entirely by hand.

A coal cutting machine was introduced at Markham in 1937, and by June 1942, conveyors were taking coal off the faces and feeding it onto gate belts. In February 1937, Markham Main was taken over by Doncaster Amalgamation Collieries Ltd.

By the 1950's Markham Main was producing 14,000 tonnes of coal a week.

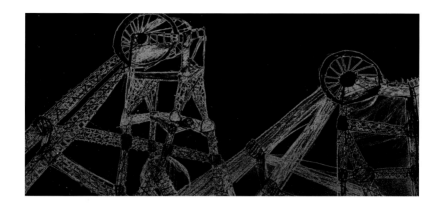

In 1973, a descending cage carrying the men down the shaft failed to slow down as it approached the bottom of the mine shaft and 18 miners were killed by the impact.

In the beginning of the 1980s the pit was producing about 24,000 tonnes of coal each week. It had three coal faces, with two coal cutting machines per face.

In 1984 the miners' strike began between the miners and the Government. Due to the strike, money became very tight and the Armthorpe community pulled together. The Baker always gave sandwiches and bread to the striking miners and their families before they started selling them to the general public. Soup kitchens became the centre of the community. The strike ended on 14th May 1985, although Markham Main didn't return to work until the 17th May.

Under British Coal Corporation, Markham made losses and, despite its substantial reserves, was closed on 16th October 1992. In 1993 the pit was described as 'non-operational'. However, it was reopened by Coal Investments Ltd in 1994. Unfortunately, heavy losses continued, and Markham finally closed in September 1996. After the closure of the mine in 1996, the area went through a deep depression.

The old colliery site is now a large housing estate and a park within a thriving community.

Written by Harvey, Khushi, Joe and Jake

DENABY-CADEBY
HISTORY

Conisbrough, previously known as Camulodunum, is situated to the south-west of Doncaster, it has one of the oldest buildings in South Yorkshire: Conisbrough Castle. This is situated in the grounds of St Peter's Church, which was built in the anglo-saxon era.

Denaby Main, previously known as Denaby Main Colliery Village, is situated in South-West Doncaster, built by Denaby Main Colliery Company, to house its workers and their families and distinguish it from the nearby village of Denaby.

Cadeby is a very small village near Conisbrough and Denaby; situated five miles west of Doncaster and four miles east of Mexborough. It is a tiny village, more like a hamlet.

Denaby Main shafts were sunk and the colliery was opened in 1856. The shafts were 409 metres in depth. Denaby Main colliery was the first colliery to be opened in Doncaster, and was owned by Waring & Company from 1856 to 1864.

In 1863, alternative employment became available when Kilner Glass opened a factory in Denaby, close to the mines. As a result of the big glassworks industry opening, more people arrived in the village. They employed up to 400 people and were producing 300,000 glass bottles a week.

In 1864, Denaby Coal Company took over the ownership of the mine, as the sinking of the shafts had been given up by Waring & Company in 1860. The company restructured itself, becoming Denaby Main Colliery Company Limited in 1868.

By 1869, Denaby Colliery had its first strike, over the management's refusal to recognise membership of the Yorkshire Miners' Association.

Other minor strikes took place in 1875 and 1877, both over wages.

On 10th July 1889, sinking of shafts for a new colliery started at Cadeby. The shafts were 687 meters in depth. In 1893, Denaby Main Colliery Company Limited opened Cadeby Main Colliery.

The 'Bag Muck Strike' started in late June 1902 because the mining company refused to pay miners for digging the muck they had to dig to get at the coal. The strike ended on 22nd March 1903. During this time, over 750 miners were evicted from their homes, as the homes they lived in were 'tied houses'.

The Cadeby Main pit disaster was a coal mining accident that occurred on the morning of 9th July 1912, at Cadeby Main Colliery, killing 88 men in total. An explosion, caused by the gases of a small fire that entered the air in the south-west part of Cadeby Main Colliery, killed 35 men. Later that day, after the rescue party was sent below ground, another explosion due to 'after damp' took place, killing 53 more men and most of the rescue party.

In 1918, Denaby and Cadeby Colliery presented Sergeant Laurence Calvert with the Victoria Cross, £300 war bonds and £25, having shown remarkable courage and devotion to duty during the First World War. He'd charged, single-handed, at the machine gun team in battle. He shot four, bayoneted three and captured two men. His actions inspired all ranks.

In 1926, an event occurred in the United Kingdom called the General Strike. The strike lasted nine days, starting on 4th May 1926. It was set up by the General Council of the Trades Union Congress, in an unsuccessful attempt to force the British government to act on wages and worsening conditions for 1.2 million locked-out coal miners. 1.7 million workers supported the strike. The strikes led to violent scenes, and the Trade Union gave up after being defeated.

In July 1935, a lightning strike on Denaby Main closed the pit for three weeks. In the same month, a roof fell on top of a miner and killed him.

In 1944, the 0.86 metres thick Beamshaw seam opened. It was worked at a depth of 578 metres until exhausted in 1966. Under the National Coal Board, the Dunsil seam was worked from 1952 until 1964, at Cadeby Main Colliery.

In 1956, Cadeby Main Colliery and Denaby Main Colliery were linked underground and coal was found and mined at the former.

The two collieries were officially and legally merged, becoming Denaby-Cadeby, on 23rd March 1968.

Denaby-Cadeby Colliery drew its last coal and closed in late 1968, due to a decline in the coal industry, but didn't get fully blocked off. Denaby's pit top remained redundant and the up-cast shaft and winder remained for emergency use, in case of any faults or disasters with the Cadeby part of the colliery. A few years later, in 1974, the Dunsil seam was re-entered at the Cadeby area of Denaby-Cadeby Colliery until geological problems were found in 1986; causing the closure of the Cadeby district of Denaby-Cadeby Colliery on 7th November 1986.

The whole site was closed shortly after the Cadeby territory of Denaby-Cadeby was closed. The year after, in 1987, the site's underground and shafts were filled in and the surface plants were cleared and demolished.

These closures led to the total rebuilding of the village. Rows of terraced houses were demolished and replaced with brand new, modern, semi-detached houses. Supermarkets and an iconic landmark known as the Earth Centre, were built; this has now become a nature reserve.

Conisbrough has a railway station and is close to motorway links.

Written by Joseph, Amardeep and Callie

ROSSINGTON
HISTORY

The name Rossington is an old Anglo-Saxon name which can be translated to 'Farm On The Moor.' There is evidence that Rossington was part of a Roman fort. Rossington is split into two parts; Old Rossington and New Rossington. New Rossington was created in 1920, for colliers and their families.

Rossington sits on the Barnsley seam, and, therefore, this was a prime location for a colliery to be built. The first shaft started to be sunk on 10th July, 1912. The shaft was 6.7 metres in diameter, although work had to stop partway through the sinking due to a large amount of flowing water. Work resumed on sinking the shaft to the Barnsley seam on 21st February 1913 and on the 3rd May 1915, the shaft was completed; reaching a depth of 798 metres. In 1915, the miners started to mine coal.

The need for workers in and around the Rossington Main colliery led to a large number of houses being built in New Rossington.

The community of Rossington was further developed by a Co-op building being built in 1915. A bus service started running in 1922 and in 1929 a cinema was created.

New Rossington pit houses and roads were developed in concentric circles around a central green; one of which stands next to a large church. It was one of the first areas in the country to have housing in concentric circles.

In 1939, Rossington pit was the first ever to have a flameproof, diesel locomotive underground. This helped move men and coal.

In 1958, Rossington railway was closed for public passenger services but was occasionally used by special trains until the mid 1960s. Rossington had its own station which was set slightly to the left of the village alongside the main road.

In 1984, the Rossington miners joined other miners at different collieries on strike against the Government's decision to close the mines.

In Rossington, during the strike, there were miners who still went to work. They were labelled 'scabs' by the picketers; a consequence of their decision to continue working. They were spat at and had bricks thrown through their house windows. If they went anywhere, they were followed all the way back to their houses.

Rossington colliery was originally closed by British Coal in 1993. It was re-opened later on in the year by UK Coal. The mine had produced 8.4 million tonnes of coal. The output that year was 518,000 tonnes; 400,000 below target. The colliery was taken over by RJB Mining. In 1994 they decided to open it again, until the final closure in 2007.

Rossington pit lay dormant for many years until the development of a multi-million pound business park called the iPort. The iPort is massive piece of land with businesses such as Amazon, Lidl and Fellowes. As part of the development 1,200 homes will be built on the old, existing pit top.

Written by Abbie, Zack and Michaela

YORKSHIRE MAIN
HISTORY

The village of Old Edlington is situated south-west of Doncaster, and is located just north of New Edlington.

In 1885, Edlington had a population of 128 people in 34 houses, farming was the village's business.

In 1907, the Staveley Coal and Iron Company, who already owned several mines, purchased the mineral rights for the whole of the Edlington area. This company bought land and the right to exploit the coal reserves under it and the adjoining land from the Cusworth Estate, between 1909 and 1910.

The first 6.6 metre shaft was sunk in 1909. The Barnsley seam was reached at a depth of 829 metres in 1911. However, when they reached the Barnsley seam, they found there was a fault where the shaft had been sunk, therefore, in 1912 the main shaft was relocated.

In 1910, New Edlington was built for the influx of new miners coming into the village for work. Edlington colliery, between 1923 and 1939, had a record output of over one million tonnes of coal.

In September 1911, the colliery changed its name to Yorkshire Main from Edlington Main.

Extraction of the Dunsil seam began in the 1950s, and the Swallow Wood seam in the 1970s. Plans had been made to open up the Parkgate seam, but these plans were abandoned with the closure of the pit.

In 1984, the longest and bitterest strike in the history of British mining began. The strike started because the Government wanted to close mines that they felt were unproductive. However, the miners did not agree with this viewpoint; including miners in Edlington.

Yorkshire Main closed in December 1985.

Written by Bobby-Jack, James and Issac

HATFIELD MAIN
HISTORY

The village of Hatfield, is situated in South Yorkshire, North East of Doncaster. Hatfield has been around since the Anglo-Saxon Period. They named the village Hetfelle and Heathfield.

In December 1910, the Hatfield Main Colliery Company was formed by Emerson Bainbridge. The first sod was cut to begin the shaft on 14th October 1911, and two shafts were simultaneously sunk. In 1917, coal was extracted from the Barnsley seam.

By 1921, Hatfield Main was in full production. The nearby railway, canal and river outlets to the Humber offered a bright view of the future for the colliery owners. In January 1927, Hatfield Main Colliery was incorporated into the Carlton Main Colliery Company, which began working the High Hazel seam.

On 12th December 1939, at 1:50pm, a problem occurred when the cage carrying the men down the shaft crashed into the headgear. One man died and 58 people were seriously injured.

In January 1947, the pit was nationalised as a colliery of the The National Coal Board which was run by the Government. Hatfield and Thorne merged to become one in 1967. In July 1973, both shafts were electrified there for they did not need steam driven engines.

The Hatfield miners played a major and central part in the 1984 Miners' strike. The strike was one of the most bitter and ferocious in living memory.

In 1992, Hatfield colliery produced 17,107 tonnes of coal from one pit face. On 3rd December 1993, British Coal stopped production at Hatfield Colliery. It cut its last piece of coal on 7th March. Hatfield Coal Co. Ltd bought out British Coal on 25th January, and started production again on 7th July 1994.

In early 2001, the pit was mothballed until October, when Coalpower Ltd, run by Richard Budge, the former owner of RJB Mining, took control of the pit.

In 2003, Coalpower Ltd published plans for a 33 hectare 'Power Park'. Geological problems at the coal face led to losses and, in late 2003, Coalpower Ltd went into administration.

Encouraged by coal prices between 2004 and 2008, Richard Budge then formed Powerfuel, to take on the colliery in 2006. A Russian coal company took a 51% stake in the venture. In 2007, the mine reopened and production started again. Thousands of miners got their jobs back and came out of debt. However, in December 2010, in part due to coal production problems, Powerfuel Mining Ltd entered administration, and in 2011, 2Co Energy Ltd. acquired the company and renamed it Hatfield Colliery Ltd. The colliery was then managed under contract by Hargreaves Services plc, who were then working Maltby colliery. An employee-controlled company, Hatfield Colliery Partnership Limited, purchased the mine in December 2013. In September 2014, a bridging loan of £4 million from the National Union of Mineworkers allowed production to be moved to a new pit face.

In 2015 the mine was closed forever, it was supposed to be closed in the summer of 2016, but due to finance issues it didn't make it that long.

The miners are planning to build a memorial. When the mine closed hundreds of people lost their jobs. Hatfield was the last deep mine in Doncaster to close down, and the second to last one in the whole of the UK.

Written by James, Milly and Henry

BENTLEY
HISTORY

Bentley is situated in the North West of Doncaster. Before the opening of the mines, Bentley was home to mostly farmland and stone houses.

In 1893, Vivian Boring Company unsuccessfully dug 563 metres at Daw Wood, only to find nine feet of coal. In March 1902, Sir William Cooke leased a large amount of land to Barber Walker & Company so they could sink the shafts. The company already had collieries in Nottinghamshire.

On the 3rd March 1906, a second shaft was sunk on a different site. It was to the west of the site originally chosen. Work began on a 7 metre diameter shaft. On the 9th October 1905, sandstone was found in the second shaft, at a depth of 15 metres. Sandstone became an increasing problem which resulted in work being stopped. On the 22nd September 1906, work on a new shaft began. By 1908, the shaft had finished being sunk. This shaft was sunk 28 metres below the Barnsley seam and 11 metres below the Dunsil seam.

By 1910, the colliery employed over a 1,000 men. The community of Bentley developed including: the development of a brass band; a successful football team and a cricket club. As the town grew, shops, parks and churches developed. Throughout the 1920's, Bentley colliery was very profitable for Barber Walker. In 1924, it was reaching its peak of production, exceeding a yearly total of over a million tonnes of coal.

Bentley was the first pit in Doncaster to install underground transport, which went over to Rossington.

On the 20th November, 1931, at 5.45pm, whilst a thousand men were working, there was a terrible firedamp explosion. Flames cascaded all around the mine, while exits were blocked by roof falls causing 45 men to lose their lives. The Barnsley seam was gassy and prone to explosions. The pit was made up of a number of separate areas that could be sealed off in case of any explosions or fires. A sufficient amount of houses were also damaged.

During 1932, Barber Walker looked to widen the coal reserves, by sinking the second shaft further than 198 metres, to confirm the Parkgate and Thorncliff seams were there. There was known to be about 1.4 and 1.5 metres of coal. This made 12,500 acres of reserves to the already-proven 6940 acres of the Barnsley seam and 6250 acres of the Dunsil seam.

Hand mining ended in 1945 due to the increase in coal faces becoming mechanised. Conveyors and skip winding were introduced in the late 1960s at Bentley, which meant the coal was brought directly from the face to the pit top with a minimum of manpower.

Between 1974 and 1982, drift mines were put up in new areas of Barnsley seam near Thorpe Marsh power station. The coal output came entirely from the Dunsil Seam which was exhausted by 1984. In the late 1980's, colliers tapped into the Parkgate seam which meant that production hit one million tonnes, annually. In December 1989, the colliery celebrated reaching a weekly best of 25,975 tonnes, and also lifting their individual tonnage record by two thirds, to 7.85 tonnes per man. They also achieved a new shift record high of 30.11 tonnes.

On the 16 November, 1993, British Coal announced its intention to close Bentley colliery. On the 3rd December, 1993, the government closed it and 450 unfortunate miners, pit nurses and colliery workers lost their jobs.

There is still a mining community in Bentley, yet there has been new, younger residents moving in. After the colliery closed, a local community school designed a nature reserve and lake next to the pit top. Shaped like a footprint, it commemorates the mine workers who lost their jobs.

Written by Alex, Ethan and Logan

AT THE COALFACE
THE PEOPLE

'I felt that in my life, I needed to do something, not to be heroic, but to help others.'

Joan Hart
Bentley Colliery

Joan Hart is an intrepid former pit nurse who dedicated her life to the mining community. After witnessing her ancestor's bravery underground, Joan believed that it was only right for her to contribute to the pit society of Bentley. Joan's occupation was one that changed the community and the world around her, and although she retired from the mines in 1987, her stories and life's work live on in her book 'At the Coalface'. She is an unrecognised heroine of the mines beneath our feet.

Joan was born in 1932 in her family home in Bentley, located in north east Doncaster. During her birth, the town of Bentley was flooded, creating pandemonium. 'The midwife had to climb into the bedroom window from a boat!' Her jovial tone indicated that from the very beginning of her life she was involved in turmoil.

Growing up, Joan's mother stayed at home and cared for the needs of her family whilst her dad and brother worked in the coal mining industry to earn money.

When Joan was only two years of age, she and her family moved from Bentley to Woodlands due to her father being connected to Brodsworth Colliery. 'My childhood was brilliant' Joan beamed. 'We used to go pea and potato picking in the summer; we'd take fresh lemonade with us too.' It is clear that from an early age Joan had a humble and unassuming personality and was inspired to pursue a similar career herself.

Joan started training at the age of sixteen, and had to spend five years working to become a fully-trained pit nurse. In 1973, she started working at Brodsworth Colliery where her father and brother already worked. However, the miners at Brodsworth were less than welcoming and seemed reluctant to accept Joan's help, and in 1974 she was commissioned at Hatfield Main Colliery.

Hatfield itself was a much more substantial colliery with three thousand men and a much larger production rate, something that may have been daunting for a new pit nurse, but for Joan it was nothing but exciting. She found that eventually she was accepted as part of the community, stating, 'They saw that I was there to help; I wasn't just another dainty little girl, I was just like them.' This shows Joan's bravery, working in an industry that was predominantly male. Joan even had to wear apple blossom perfume when going down the shafts to help. If she didn't, they wouldn't recognise her.

'They saw that I was there to help – I wasn't just another dainty little girl, I was just like them.'

Joan had to show immense courage when facing difficult situations. 'The only hard thing was having to go to a miner's house and explain the death of their loved one.'

Joan wasn't affected by the 1972 blackout, due to living in London with her husband. Shortly after returning from London, she started working at Bentley Colliery. Joan lived and worked through the Bentley pit disaster as well as the 1984 miners' strike. According to Joan, the strikes were the worst years of her career. The pit nurses were required to go to work despite the ongoing strikes, and as a result, were stoned and spat on by those at the picket lines. Joan herself had to be escorted to the medical centre by police officers, and when they were there, they were required to continue helping the miners who went to work.

In the midst of the strike, with Christmas looming, Joan and her colleagues decided that they should do something to help the striking families, especially those with young children. 'We gathered old shoeboxes and filled them with toys, notebooks, teddies and colouring pencils.' Joan thought that they couldn't use old things, they needed to buy proper presents from the shops for their project.

On the 23rd December, the boxes were left on the doorsteps of hundreds of miners' homes, with a Merry Christmas cards to go with it. 'We were in a community, and everyone cared for each other', said Joan.

After the strike was over, Joan continued work and watched the pit community gradually be rebuilt, but it was never the same as it used to be. 'The spirit was lost.' Joan concedes, 'there was something before that strike that I didn't think would ever come back.'

Joan and her colleagues continued work, and even went as far as adopting a puppy: Noel. Joan had discovered Noel one morning when she found a little bundle outside the medical centre door. She found the Border Terrier inside and, after calling the police to find there were no claims, she took Noel into her care. From then on, the nurses at the medical centre looked after Noel. But when Bentley Colliery closed down, Joan was forced to send Noel into the care of someone else as she already had two cats at home. At Christmas, Joan received a call from the worker who owned Noel. 'It turns out that Noel was a girl, and she'd had puppies at Christmas Eve!' Joan chuckled.

- -

'The spirit was lost. There was something before that strike that I didn't think would ever come back.'

- -

'It hardly exists any more – it's so sad, the heart of Doncaster's gone.'

In 1978, a horrific disaster occurred at Bentley Colliery. There were seven casualties, all from one paddy train. Joan was famously the first person underground to help, and to witness the horrific scene. Struggling to speak about it she states. 'At first I thought it was just a little accident' She says. 'But then I heard what had happened. It was unspeakable.' Joan's change in demeanor indicated that she is reluctant to allow the memories of Bentley back. She saved many of the miners down there, but there were those who were beyond help.

Joan retired as a pit nurse 1987, and then began working in Doncaster Royal Infirmary. She spent several years volunteering at Cancer Research, and she recently went wing walking and free falled! Twice! Now, Joan visits schools to share her stories and inspire those who listen. Her book, at the coalface, was a huge success with the help of ghost writer Veronica Clarke.

Joan recently visited our school to share with us her stories and life's work. Overall, Joan's acts of courage and kindness have made a lasting impact on many miners' lives, teaching us that you can achieve whatever you want if you are passionate and put your mind to it. Joan's actions and bravery has inspired us and our peers, showing us that each and every community holds something special.

Written by Jon and Anisa

Aggie Curry
Markham Main

Aggie Currie is a strong-willed, independent woman, who played a significant part in the miners' strike. She is a person who is soft on the inside, but tough when she needs to be. Aggie devoted her life to the Armthorpe community, and sought to find justice for the miners.

Aggie was born in 1950, in the mining community of Armthorpe. Aggie had a 'normal childhood, but far from luxurious'. She is the middle child and explained how she was always given responsibilities stating, 'it was always me who was asked to help out; like go and collect the coal.' It was obvious from talking to Aggie that she has always had strong leadership qualities. People relied on her, even from a very young age.

When Aggie was older, she was very pleased that her country had its first, female Prime-Minister, Margaret Thatcher, but those feelings were lost when Thatcher tore apart the mining community.

Aggie didn't want to be a part of the strike, and wasn't interested until a lady invited her to a meeting about how women could become the backbone of the strike. At the beginning of the strike, Aggie outlined that the 'community spirit was fairly high, and everyone had trust in each other.' Even without an income and lack of most necessities. She spoke emotionally about how the community has changed, stating 'nowadays there is no community spirit, nobody knows people on their street like they used to.'

Aggie recalls Christmas being one of the hardest times for the community, as everything was financially hard and people were worried. 'We didn't have a Christmas tree that year, so I went into next door's garden and cut their tree down. I knew it wasn't the right thing to do, but I couldn't bare to see my children disappointed. My neighbour forgave me. They knew what we were going through. That's what I mean by community spirit.' This showed that all families would look out for each other and wanted to see their community happy.

'We didn't have a Christmas tree that year so I went into next door's garden and cut their tree down. I knew it wasn't the right thing to do, but I couldn't bare to see my children disappointed. My neighbour forgave me. They knew what we were going through. That's what i mean by community spirit.'

Aggie found her life extremely difficult during the strike, she got arrested seventeen times, but never prosecuted. This had a massive impact on her family, especially her daughter, who found refuge by writing poetry about her mother and the strike. Aggie became tearful as she recalled a time when her daughter became unwell, and she desperately needed to stay warm. Aggie explained how her determination to care for her children led her to 'sneaking into someone else's house, grabbing a bag full of coal, looking for an open door and then running straight through it.' It was due to her determination, courage and occasionally ruthless nature, that Aggie ended up taking a lead role in the fight against Margaret Thatcher and pit closures.

Aggie currently works as Service Supervisor at the Royal Infirmary in Doncaster. She is an active member of the community, and still lives in Armthorpe. Aggie, reflecting on her life, encouraged us to travel and make the most of life, stating, 'There is a big world out there; a world I wish I could see. Study hard, make the most of your education and make wise choices.'

Through Aggie's stories and life, we have been able to understand how much the miners gave to the community of Doncaster and how important it is that we remember them. We would like to give our sincere thanks to Aggie for giving up her valuable time to share her life's journey with us.

Written by Gracie and Chandni

Frank Arrowsmith
Yorkshire Main

Frank Arrowsmith is a courageous and determined man who has devoted his life to the mining industry. Working as an official at Yorkshire Main Colliery, he became a strong figure of his community. Frank is full of amusing and interesting stories about his experience of the turmoil that was the miners' strike and how this affected his life and those surrounding him.

Frank left school at the age of fifteen without any qualifications after a terrible experience of education. A few short weeks later, he found himself working alongside his extended family on the pit site. This was no surprise to Frank, as it was a family tradition. An expectation. 'Like a grown-up world at only fifteen' he stated. When Frank first started working he was incredibly nervous due to the fact that he knew nobody there except his family, and he could get badly injured.

Having secured the job, he began the induction period. First he had to pass a medical examination. Once he was considered well enough he was shadowed by a supervisor for twenty days until he was competent and confident enough to go down the mines by himself. 'I'll always remember that day, because he frightened me, he did.' Frank explained. 'I knew I needed to work hard and not let my family down. It was a great job, a great opportunity.'

Frank's father worked as a miner and his mother and wife were both integral to the mining community.

Frank was actively involved in the strike, organising protests all over Doncaster. He also travelled all around the country to picket for other communities. To take part in the picket lines, you had to be a strong member with a determined heart, as it was tough to participate in. Frank was even involved in the Battle of Orgreave, which he refused to label as a battle.

'I didn't see Orgreave as a battle, because a battle is when there are two sides fighting each other, but it was just the police fighting us.'

During the strike, the miners were so desperate for supplies, some of them actually sneaked over to the pit tops and stole sizeable lumps of coal for their heating. 'After all', he added, 'we're the ones that dug it all up in the first place.' The miners also had their own little saying: 'A miner's most important duties; keep your family warm, keep your family fed.' The tone of Frank's voice, as he recalled this, showed how dedicated he was to his family. So much so, that he was willing to do anything to keep himself and his family safe, warm and fed.

In 1985, the strike ended and the miners reluctantly returned back to work. Margaret Thatcher had won. However, Frank didn't go back to work, he stayed at home, still bitter and angry from the outcome of the strike.

Many ex-miners celebrated the death of Thatcher. Frank and his family were some of those people. 'Did I celebrate Margaret Thatcher's death? Ooh... Yes! Yes I did.' Arrowsmith and his friends and family were so pleased at Thatcher's death, they threw a party. 'I would look at Thatcher as someone who cost me my job and ruined my life.' Frank believed that Margaret Thatcher demolished his community.

We also consulted Frank on our guiding question: What does the community of Doncaster owe to the miners? Frank answered, 'I think the the community owes a lot to the miners, because we have done so much toward Doncaster, as well as other places. Our work could have changed the world.' He was boasting now, recalling the work he'd done in his time.

- -

I think the the community owes a lot to the miners, because we have done so much toward Doncaster, as well as other places. Our work could have changed the world.'

- -

Frank worked down the mine for 45 years and later went on to become a Trade Union official; helping to organise local mini-strikes supported by the public. He retired at the age of 60 after a long career devoted to the mining industry. Frank has remained a strong and influential member of his community and has been an amazing inspiration. At present, he has stuck to his responsibility of leading people by taking on the challenge of being the Deputy Mayor of Edlington.

Frank has helped us understand what it was like to be a miner, especially during the strike. Finally, we would like to show our appreciation to Frank for his honesty, his courage and for taking the time to talk us about his life. We will never forget the Miners' Strike of 1984; it was a significant part of UK's history. Let us learn from those that have lived before us and be thankful for all they have done.

Written by Emilly-Mae and Thomas

Ruth Johnson
Rossington Colliery

Ruth Johnson is a resilient woman with many life experiences to share. She speaks openly about how such experiences, like the miners' strike, impacted her family and shaped her into the person she is today.

Ruth Johnson was born in 1965 in Durham. Ruth is an active person and commented how her childhood revolved around sport. 'I lived and breath sports.' During her childhood her father worked down the mines, whilst her mother stayed at home to take care of the family and household. Ruth remembers fondly how her mother would take her to the colliery gates quite regularly, so that she could go and collect her father's wages from the window. Her father would then show her around the shower area. Ruth smiles 'he would let us try on the miner's helmet, so we enjoyed going to visit.'

After six years of living in Durham, Ruth and her family moved to Rossington, due to pit closures. Ruth lived there until she got married to a miner and moved to the nearby village of Harworth.

Ruth was just eighteen years old when she got married, and this was in the midst of the strike. When Ruth got married, her father-in-law didn't fully accept her, but they still carried on with the wedding. She said 'My ex-husband's father didn't agree with the strike, so he didn't contribute to the wedding. I had to buy my own wedding dress.'

As the wedding went on, the two families didn't communicate with each other. One family on one side and the other family on the other. This was because Ruth's father was a deputy and a striking miner, and Ruth's father-in-law was against the strike.

- -

'My ex-husband's father didn't agree with the strike, so he didn't contribute to the wedding. I had to buy my own wedding dress.'

- -

Ruth's husband didn't agree with the miners' strike, and decided to return back to work. This meant he was a target for abuse and hate from the striking miners in his community. Ruth states, 'it was a really difficult time for everyone'.

After the strike, Ruth's husband was a contractor and was transferred from Rossington to a Nottingham Colliery. Ruth's youngest son was subject to bullying because of his father's decision to work during the strike. Ruth was emotional as she explained the effect on her children. Stating 'it had a huge effect on them, school life was very challenging and often they were called hurtful names.'

We asked Ruth our Guiding Question of 'What does the community of Doncaster owe to the miners?' She responded, 'the community owe a lot to the miners because the miners have sacrificed their lives for us and to develop our world and communities.' She went on to say, 'we need to remember the hard work people put into coal mining and the benefits we have reaped from it.' Ruth explained how in her old community of Rossington there is now a memorial garden to show respect to the miners.

Currently, Ruth is a learning coach at XP school in Doncaster. Despite how hard it was to grow up in the midst of the miners' strike, she said, 'I think the strike has shaped me into the person I am today, stronger and more determined'. We would like to thank Ruth for taking the time to speak openly about her life.

Written by Jaspreet and Jack

Rachel Horne
Denaby-Cadeby Colliery

Rachel Horne grew up in the mining community of Conisbrough, where four generations of her family had devoted their lives to the mining industry. Rachel was born during the 1984 miners strike and produces artwork expressing her thoughts on the mines.

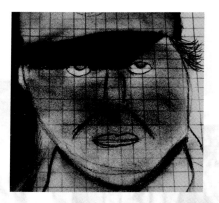 

Rachel was born in the mining community of Conisbrough in 1984, in the midst of the chaotic strike. Commenting on her childhood, Rachel stated, 'we weren't an affluent family, which meant that we didn't have much, but I had a great childhood.' Rachel explained how her mother looked after her whilst her father worked down the pit at Cadeby Colliery.

Rachel loved her community and stated 'it was very strong, everyone knew everyone and looked out for everyone.' As the strike went on Margaret Thatcher was being portrayed by the miners as a 'wicked witch.' Rachel's family didn't like her and described her as a 'nasty piece of work'. One of the songs chanted at the time was 'Here's Maggie Thatcher throw her up and catch her, squish squash squish squash, dead Maggie Thatcher'.

On one family outing, Rachel and some of her friends got some seaweed and pretended it was Margaret Thatcher. They smashed it against the rocks on the beach to show they really hated her, although they didn't realise at the time exactly who she was.

Although she grew up during the strike, it wasn't until she was a young adult that she understood the complexities of it all.

In 2002, at the age of eighteen, Rachel moved to London. Due to her passion for art, she wanted to start a career as an artist and she thought the capital city, with it's galleries and lifestyle, would be the best place for this.

However, the main reason she moved away was to get her career started and, eventually, bring her work back to her hometown of Doncaster.

While she was in London she studied the history of the subjects that she wanted to include in her artwork, which turned out to be mining.

'Every one is an artist, even if you don't think you are.'

Rachel came back from London seven years later as she wanted to learn more about what happened historically in Conisbrough. Her aim was to focus on portraying the complexities of the mining strike through her artwork. It was only through studying for her art work that she was able to fully grasp what happened and why miners were so angry.

At present, Rachel is working in her own popular showcase museum in Doncaster town centre. She is still in touch with some of her dad's friends from the mines. They have aided her with her work, explaining about what has happened to the community after the mines closed. We would like to thank Rachel for taking the time to share with us her work and her life.

Written by Tabitha, Megan and Sam

Tom Burns
Bentley Colliery

Tom Burns is a courageous, kind man, who devoted his life to the mining industry as a methane borer. Whilst working in his late career, Tom had an accident which affected his life significantly.

Tom was born on 2nd December 1962, into a typical mining community. He recalls his childhood fondly: 'brilliant childhood, absolutely brilliant... in the summer I played football everyday... none of that internet, mostly outside me house.' He explained how life was simple and happy, until he reached his teens, and then the fear and apprehension of a working life as a miner crept in.

After seeing what his dad did, Tom followed in his footsteps to become a miner. He started by training in several collieries across Doncaster. Once the training process was over, Tom became a Methane Borer. Tom had three different types of shifts: day shift, afters and nights. Tom would work one type of shift, 7 days a week, switching every week on a rotation. He worked every day of every month, of every year, until the strike occurred. He worked for just over 7 hours a day. Sometimes, Tom stated, that he 'got paid double, maybe even triple, more than his friends.' You could tell from the smile on his face that this delighted him. A lot of the time, he would get offered bonuses if more methane was found, this was one of the reasons Tom was always a methane borer in the mining industry.

- -

'I really embraced and enjoyed the camaraderie of the underground community. You could trust nearly anybody in the close knit community of the pit – I had loads of close friends.'

- -

As a result of Margaret Thatcher's intentions to close the mine, Tom, as well as many other miners, went on strike for a full year. He told us that 'he wasn't surprised that Margaret Thatcher tried to close the mines', instead he 'felt bitter.' With the termination of the mines, Tom claimed that he had, 'Absolutely no respect of her (Margaret Thatcher) whatsoever!' No job, meant no money. The only income they were receiving was his mother's. However, Tom and his father did receive one pound a day for picketing. Tom missed his job but never considered crossing the picket line.

Finally, on the 3rd March 1985, the strike ended, and the miners reluctantly returned to work. However, after the strike, Tom feels that 'if Scargill had held the battle, it wouldn't have gone the same way.'

On June 11th 1994, Tom Burns had a traumatic accident that could have cost him his life. Whilst he was working, a paddy train spliced into the side of his foot. Tom had never had an accident in any other collieries across Doncaster. This would be his first, and his first would be a memorable one.

Once Tom had been hit by the paddy train, he said he could see, 'a red line coming off of my foot,' and, 'flesh hanging off of my boot.' He was not found immediately; instead, despite the pain, he just covered it up and carried on walking. This proved how courageous he could be. 'It took 15 minutes for someone to get to me.' Tom then had to go to hospital for six months and was treated to a Chinese flap.

This meant he had to wear special shoes. However, they made him insecure stating, 'I felt self aware. It felt like everyone was looking at me.'

Tom also has a 'syringe driver' which sends signals to his brain to stop the pain in his foot but can only be switched on at night because it, 'completely knocks me out.' After the treatment was over, Tom found that he was left with half a tattoo on his right foot, and a dint in his arm. This was from where they'd took the nerves and flesh off, which they then connected to his foot. In addition to this, Tom had two years off work. He was tremendously brave to carry on working. Tom believes that the overall experience was a massive eye-opener.

Shortly following Tom's incident, the mines started to close and it wasn't long before Tom's pit shut down. At first, Tom was very bitter when the government started closing the mines, because they'd said that they would only close mines not making a profit. Bentley, at the time, was making a colossal profit of sixty million. Tom said, 'there's still sixty million tonnes of coal down that mine.' Due to the closure, communities were broken and families lost jobs. Tom felt that the respect of the underground community was lost. Everything changed for Tom after this point.

'If Scargill had held the battle, it wouldn't have gone the same way.'

A few years ago, Tom took up a training course to be a forklifter. He now has a new occupation and works as a warehouse operative in Doncaster. Whilst talking with Tom, he answered the question, 'what does the community of Doncaster owe to the miners?' Tom thought about this then passionately stated, 'I think Doncaster owes everything to the miners, and because of this, I think there should be more of a memorial to them.'

Tom has taught us many things about the mining community and the life of a miner. We would like to thank him for giving up his time to educate us on the mining industry and the effects of the strike on our community.

Written by Scarlett and Jac

Mick Lanaghan
Hatfield Main

Mick Lanaghan is an ex-miner who has devoted his life to Hatfield Colliery. Even after suffering a horrific spine injury, he was determined that he would continue to work in the mining industry. Mick's life has been full of challenging times. He pulled through due to both his incredible belief and also how he was inspired, by his father, to never give up and stand his ground.

Mick was born on the 1st October 1959, into a traditional Irish Catholic family. He was a miner and was immensely proud of it too. He loved the community that he grew up in, and mentioned that his father never wanted him to go down the mine. However, Mick was determined. He said he knew it was only a matter of time before he followed in his father's footsteps. Eventually, Mick faced his father, explaining how he was inspired to work down the pit.

At the age of seventeen, after much persuasion, his father agreed to let him work down the mine. Before he began working, he had to take a two-month training course at Bentley Colliery. After which, he began working at Hatfield Main.

Following this, he became a belt maintenance worker, where he had to ensure all the conveyer belts were in perfect condition. Later on, Mick then went back to Bentley, to have two months of coal face training before returning to Hatfield, where he actually became a miner. From what Mick has said, the training was very important and of an extremely high standard. He thought that mining was an excellent job, since you got good training before starting work.

When Mick first began working, he was amazed at how many little things could cause explosions, including the tins from pies that some miners took down the pit for their lunch. During his time at the pit, for him, the greatest privilege was the five years he spent as a spokesperson for his fellow miners.

When he did this, he had everyone behind him. Mick had a lot of responsibility on his shoulders, as he was chosen to represent his fellow colleagues. Mick Lanaghan helped to bring everyone together. He and his work colleagues all stuck with each other, especially during the strike.

After many years working down the pit, Mick had an horrific accident that could have cost him his life. All he knows about the incident is what his friends have told him. In the mine, he was on an underground train, when suddenly a massive chunk of rock fell on the carriage that he was in. The roof was crushed from the weight of the boulder, and Mick was sent flying back against the wall, where his spine was instantly fractured. At this time, worrying thoughts rushed through his head, he didn't know what state he would be left in.

After the accident, Mick became a safety inspector. His job was to check and make sure everything was safe and in working condition.

Following this, Margaret Thatcher announced the pit closures which caused the devastating strike of 1984-85 to occur. Of course, like most miners, he hated Thatcher's guts and would stop at nothing to halt her plans.

When he found out that Thatcher was trying to close down the pits, he ran home and cried, which just shows how important the mines were and still are to him and his fellow miners. When Mick's beloved pit closed he was upset for the mine, and upset for his work colleagues.

In the present, Hatfield Main is still here, just not a running mine anymore.

Mick Lanaghan is a strong and determined individual, who believes in good. He now works at Hatfield Main Heritage Association. He has taught us that we wouldn't be where we are now without the miners.

- -

'They played a crucial role in the history of our country, so we should not forget them, but honour them.'

- -

Written by Charlotte and Rex

Dennis Nowell
Markham Main Colliery

Dennis Nowell, a 77 year old ex-blacksmith, shares with us the incredible and heroic stories of his adventures, saving lives and risking his own in the unstoppable darkness. A real hero.

Born in 1939, in the village of Armthorpe, Dennis grew up in a disadvantaged family, with parents who had low income occupations. His mother was a cleaner and his father was a miner. As a result of his parent's low yearly income, he only received a minimal set of gifts for Christmas. In fact, this consisted of a pillowcase, containing an apple, an orange, and sometimes a pear. However, this was completely normal for him, as it was what he grew up with.

As a boy, his mother wanted him to attend ballet. However, Dennis was reluctant. Eventually, he went, and to his astonishment, he loved it. Later he tried tap dancing and the outcome was the same. As you can tell, young Dennis already led quite an interesting life. As well as dance, he, like many other boys, enjoyed sports at school. He told us that he enjoyed school immensely and he repeatedly advised us to 'work hard at school and get a good education, grasp it with both hands.'

Dennis started work in 1954 at the age of fifteen. However, he wasn't a blacksmith. He was a painter and decorator, working from early in the morning until late at night. His hard labour was not reflected in his wages. He told us his wage was the equivalent of £20.18 in the present day. Now, jobless, his mum advised him to become a miner, as they got paid a reasonable amount. Listening to his mother's advice Dennis started work at Armthorpe Colliery. He worked for one week in a training facility, and another week with an experienced miner, undergoing basic training.

Once qualified, he started work at the tub shop, transporting coal out of the mine. A few months after this, he was given the opportunity to train and work within the mining company, as a blacksmith.

This marked a significant change in Dennis' life and career. He repeatedly said that being a blacksmith was 'very heavy work'. We think that being a blacksmith is a difficult job as you have to understand the process from material to goods.

Dennis and his colleagues made everything from horseshoes to rail junctions. As a result of mining, Dennis is partially deaf in his left ear and he has got a condition called 'White Finger' which many ex-blacksmiths have. Dennis said 'It was only when I went to a power station at Barnby Dun, and I dropped something, and this bloke said, 'Do you know what that is?', I said no. He said 'that's White Finger, have you used pneumatic tools?' I said I have, so that's why my fingers are white.' This shows the emotional and physical strains of the job on Dennis.

Another word I would use to describe Dennis is 'hero', as he has saved the lives of children and miners. He saved a young girl's life in Skegness, when she was on a scooter and fell over the handlebars. Luckily Dennis had trained at a civil defense unit. He knew how to give CPR and, luckily, was passing by at the time. The girl was turning blue and Dennis screamed in her ear to try and get her to wake her up. He thumped her on the back and she exhaled suddenly and sharply, saving her life. 'I could see that she was turning blue, so I started screaming in her ear.'

Another example of Dennis' bravery was at Markham Main Colliery. He was working down the mine repairing a piece of machinery and heard a soft 'help.' He said that the wind must have been blowing in just the right direction for him to hear. He went running with a few other miners to what they thought was the source of the sound. He sprinted ahead and ran under the support beams, which held up the big carts full of coal. He smashed his head on one of the beams. 'My eye were out here' he said with an outstretched arm, 'but I kept going.' He ran further, to the creepers, where the coal carts tipped the coal out. Somehow a young man had fallen and got his leg caught in the rollers. Heroically, Dennis pulled a lever which stopped the carts moving and freed the man. If Dennis had not been there, the man would have been crushed in seconds. Dennis told me 'that lad regularly came to the workshop and thanked me for his life.'

Since retiring from mining, Dennis has created a memorial garden that is a legacy to the miners who live, and who have fallen. We understood the passion that he held for his garden, through how fondly he discussed it. He made it to honour the men who gave their lives for coal, and he believes that they should always be remembered. We went to visit the garden, and we could see and feel the hard work and dedication that went in to make it and maintain it.

Dennis describes being down the pit as being in an 'endless night'. We think that this is a beautiful comment. Dennis has been sponsored by many people to achieve this garden and make his dream come true. He is currently building a new garden on the site of the mine, and he has high ambitions for who will unveil it. He's asked the Queen!

We would describe Dennis as a strong-willed man with a huge heart. He is grateful for what he is given. We think that people now have lost that. We always want more than what we have, and never stop to appreciate the world and what we have in it. We think that we should all be more like Dennis Nowell. A truly inspirational man.

Written by Sureya and Anna

Louise Harrison
Campaigner

Louise Harrison is a fearless and independent woman who grew up surrounded by the mayhem of the miners' strike. The strike started when Louise was a teenager, and she recalls how such experiences have influenced her outlook on life.

Louise Harrison was born in the village of Askern in 1970. Her father worked as a miner following his redundancy. The family were provided with a house because of her father's contributions to the industry. She explained, 'sometimes they had to be quiet during the day because my dad worked night shifts.' Her mum worked as a catering assistant at the local primary school, where she attended. Louise struggled at school academically, recalling 'I remember trying to avoid mathematics lessons.' However, at school she always enjoyed playing sports, and socialising which was a big part of her life. She explained how playing sports was key as it helped her confidence grow.

Louise explained how Margaret Thatcher was admired at first, because she was the first female Prime Minister, but that soon changed. In 1984, after five years of her dad working down the pit, Margaret Thatcher and the Conservative government announced job redundancies and colliery closures. This resulted in the miners striking against the Conservatives, as they wanted to save their jobs.

Louise's initial thought was that the strike would not impact on her very much. She imagined that life would carry on as normal, not realising that everything would change. After a while, people started to get agitated and anxious; these feelings started to spread around the whole community, then the country. By the time this happened, the strike had impacted other industries throughout the country, such as power plants and steel works.

Louise and her family were big supporters of Arthur Scargill, the leader of the National Union of Mineworkers. Louise stated, 'he never told lies and he always told the truth.' She felt he truly believed in what the miners were fighting for.

The strike was a major part of Louise's life. It affected her and her family in a significant way. Louise's mum worked in a soup kitchen and also started to join the picket lines. Her mother got involved in protesting during the strike, in support of the miners, and Louise eventually joined her and participated in these events. Louise explained that her favourite part of her protesting experience was when she went down to London and saw all the different stalls which argued on behalf of different types of campaigns. 'It was an eye opening and exciting experience for me.'

The strike meant that families were struggling financially and families struggled to buy proper food, so they had to get used to living on bread, water and soup.

'The strike strengthened the community as everyone pulled together.'

There had been a lot of miners under house arrest to stop them picketing, but that didn't stop the women fighting for their husbands rights.

That year, Louise only had one dress, and was given some money to go to the pictures. The strike affected the miner's wages. However, she didn't mind, as she knew her Dad was not being paid during the strike, and that times were hard. They all had to work together as a family.

- -

'You didn't know when you'd get your next meal.'

- -

That year she learnt something important. 'It's not about protecting yourself, it's about looking after your family." Things also became different at home. Her father was the one to mainly care for the children, while her mother was working in the soup kitchen or protesting.

Louise was on her way back to the village from a birthday treat to Cleethorpes with friends of the family, when she heard on the news that the strike had ended. People knew that there would be changes in the community, because the miners had lost their battle with the government. They knew that some of the mines would now be closed down and people would lose their jobs and their homes. The community had supported each other throughout this tough time, but now they started to feel lost again and depressed.

Unfortunately, at the age of seventeen, Louise's parents announced they were divorcing. She blamed the strike as part of the cause for this, although when they split up, it helped her to become more independent.

Louise left home with her newfound independence and embarked on a degree studying social politics. Following this, she took on the job of working for a women's charity and has since won several awards for her contributions towards campaigns.

Currently, Louise still actively campaigns for women's rights. Recently one of her arguments was posted on Left Unity Politics, with the headline of 'Left Unity's modest flutter: A response'. In this, Louise talked about her background and how this had led to her to campaign for women's rights.

'One of the most important things that came from the strike is that women have gained more respect by working alongside the men.'

We would like to thank Louise for being so open in speaking about her life and sharing her personal journey into women's rights. Following her visit to our school we feel that she has affected our view of life in a major way, and spoke to us inspirationally; educating us on the miners' strike through the eyes of a child who lived through it.

Written by Tyler and Liam

WHAT DOES THE COMMUNITY OF DONCASTER OWE TO THE MINERS?

The community of Doncaster owes so much to the miners.

In 1984 they sacrificed a year of providing for their families to fight against the pit closures. The resilience that they drew from their community meant that the strike lasted much longer than anyone anticipated. The communities fought for what they believed was right.

'If they had no sugar then we had no sugar.'
Aggie Currie

This quotation is by Aggie describing how the community pulled together and helped each other in their time of need. Members of the community even did two grocery shops, one for themselves and one for the miners. This demonstrates just how much people thought they owed to the miners at that time.

Without the miners, in the last couple of hundred years, people would not have been able to keep warm. In the early 1900 the UK was heavily reliant on coal to keep the country going. So, without the miners, the last 200 years would have been cold and dark. We owe the miners our thanks for keeping the country going, and making us prosperous during the industrial revolution and following years.

Lots of the jobs that people held were, in some way, a consequence of the mining industry. It provided jobs for other people in associated industries and business, as well as themselves. For example, the miners needed equipment so other people could work in supplying helmets. The miners needed torches; every mine needed torches. They would break often so the demand for torches was high. This meant that other people had jobs.

In Doncaster in particular, the rail and coal industry grew in tandem. Doncaster became more connected to the rest of the country through rail, and in turn the coal mined in Doncaster helped fuel the railways and their expansion.

Doncaster owes nearly everything to those workers. Underground, they drove the early days of industry in Yorkshire for little more than a couple of pennies in return. So many men risked their lives down there, many paying the ultimate price.

Above all, we owe miners our respect. Respect for being the only people who were willing to go down into darkness to light our country. Respect for living on the bare minimum for one day short of a year to fight for theirs and other people's jobs. Respect for picking themselves up after their whole community was destroyed; they were jobless, they had families to feed, they had bills to pay and they had Christmas presents to buy.

'Since the mines shut, its almost like Doncaster had a huge earthquake that broke communities and families apart.'

Rachel Horne

Since the mines closed there can be no doubt that the community spirit in the areas around each pit has diminished. We owe it to the miners to bring this community spirit back, by working hard together and by showing compassion to our neighbours.

The community of Doncaster owes so much to the miners. Without them, the Doncaster that we know today would be unrecognisable. Doncaster's mining past is something of which we are all a part. It is up to us to continue to tell the miners' stories to ensure that we uphold Doncaster's legacy as a mining town.

We owe them everything.